James A. Edwards

Napoleon Bonaparte

Was He the Man of Popular History?

.

James A. Edwards

Napoleon Bonaparte
Was He the Man of Popular History?

ISBN/EAN: 9783337350444

Printed in Europe, USA, Canada, Australia, Japan

Cover: Foto ©ninafisch / pixelio.de

More available books at **www.hansebooks.com**

NAPOLEON BONAPARTE

Was he the Man of Popular History?

BY

JAMES AUGUSTUS EDWARDS

PRINTED FOR PRIVATE CIR-
CULATION AT THE LAKESIDE
PRESS, CHICAGO, MDCCCXCIX

TO MY WIFE

NAPOLEON BONAPARTE

WAS HE THE MAN OF POPULAR HISTORY?

It is greatly to be regretted that the character of Napoleon Bonaparte is so misunderstood and generally condemned. History does not contain a personage so fascinating and at the same time more interesting, about whom there is such a diversity of opinion.

That this is so, is largely due to the English, who pursued him with relentless hatred, misrepresenting his character, ridiculing his motives, and finally contributing more largely than any other nation to his downfall.

The exaggerated statements of his enemies were received with avidity, and, where it was possible, enlarged upon and given the greatest publicity by the press, and from

repeated reiterations finally became accepted
as historical facts, and were and are to this
day used in most accounts of his life. It is
from these that the general reader has
formed his or her opinion, and while time
has discovered many official documents and
much private correspondence which stamp
most of these so-called anecdotes and acts
as without foundation, gradually a clearer
conception of his character is becoming
more possible; nevertheless, as is usually
the case, the contradiction of a statement is
never given the same publicity or as widely
read as is the original statement, especially
where a wrong is to be corrected; therefore,
it is not as generally known that these reports
were the "invention of the enemy."

Again, Napoleon is placed at a great dis-
advantage by being judged from a nineteenth-
century standpoint. Is it not absolutely
impossible after a lapse of a hundred years
of unprecedented advancement in science,
literature and art, to calmly sit in judgment
on Napoleon's motives and intentions, and

give him a fair trial? Would it not be more just to compare him with his contemporaries, Alexander I of Russia, Francis II of Austria, Frederick William III of Prussia, and George IV of England, taking into consideration the conditions and traditions of the times, and, what is equally important, the condition of the people, both morally and intellectually? It should be borne in mind that Napoleon appeared on the scene of action, following the profligate reign of Louis XV and the degenerate reign of Louis XVI, at a time that made the French Revolution a possibility, and later, a stern reality; when the army was the power behind the throne, whose influence was overwhelming; when law was trampled under foot and set at defiance by the King and his courtiers. To these, life was a long holiday of riotous pleasure and voluptuousness. Religion had become a byword and jest, and it was the fashion to be both a scoffer and an unbeliever. The people had no rights that were respected, and

finally new indignities and additional taxa-
tion being more than they could bear, after
years of suffering they rebelled.   One
extreme followed another; in proportion to
the severity with which they had been held
in bondage, in the same ratio did they riot
when liberated by the Revolution.   How
true it is, that in the times of the greatest
emergencies in the histories of the various
nations, when law and order seemed threatened with annihilation, nature appears to
have foreseen the crisis, and to have fur-
nished characters that restored peace and
brought order out of chaos.   Such were
Cromwell, Washington, Napoleon and Lin-
coln.   How often we have heard the ques-
tion: " How was France benefited by Napoleon?"   Did he not give her a religion, and
force her to respect it?   Did he not give to
France and the world the Code Napoleon?
Both of these great undertakings were
accomplished in ten years.   Can we recall
another ruler, either before or since, that
accomplished more?   Since it is impossible

for us to retrocede a century and judge with the same feelings as of that time, let us consult a few of his contemporaries, and if possible from their opinions derive more light as to the character of the man, rather than the monarch; and let us hope that in time posterity will give to Napoleon the credit that is due him, and perceive that he was richly endowed with the milk of human kindness, but that on account of the peculiar position he occupied, was not permitted at all times to give vent to his better feelings. I make no pretensions to independent or original research, but simply wish to lay before you briefly the opinion of a number of authorities, some of whom, on account of their close connections with Napoleon, cannot be passed over lightly, and which it is hoped will be of interest.

The following is from Henri Taine's remarkable essay on Napoleon:

" He is not only out of the common run, but there is no standard of measurement for him ; through his temperament, instincts, faculties, imagination, passions, and moral constitution, he seems cast in a different mould, composed of another metal than that which enters into a composition of his fellows and contemporaries. Evidently, he is not a Frenchman, nor a man of the eighteenth century; he belongs to another race and another epoch; we detect in him, at the first glance, the foreigner, the Italian, and something more apart and beyond these, surprising all similitude and analogy. Extraordinary and superior, made to command and to conquer."

Madame de Staël says: "Every time I heard him talk I was struck with his superiority and soon found that his character was not to be described in terms commonly employed."

Roeder (Deputy) who saw Bonaparte daily at the meetings of the Council of State, and who noted every evening the impressions of the day, says: "Punctual at every sitting, prolonging the sessions five or six hours, discussing before and afterward

the subjects brought forward, always returning to two questions, 'Is that *just?* Is that
useful?' Never did the Council adjourn
without its members knowing more than the
day before."

Following is an extract from Josephine to
her daughter, Hortense:

" How could you conceive that I partici-
pate in such ridiculous, or, perhaps, malicious
opinions? No! you do not think that I believe you to be my rival. We, indeed, both
reign in the same bosom, though by very
different, yet equally sacred right, and they
who, in the affection which my husband
manifests for you, have pretended to dis-
cover other sentiments than those of a parent
and a friend, know not his soul. His is a
mind too elevated above the vulgar ever to
be accessible to the passions. That of glory,
if you will, engrosses him too entirely for
our repose, but at least glory inspires nothing vile. Such are my professions of faith."

Extracts from a letter written by Josephine to the Countess de Girardin:

"The Emperor, indignant at the total disregard of morality, and alarmed at the
progress it might still make, is resolved that
the example of a life of regularity and of
religion shall be given in the palace where
he commands, desirous of strengthening
more and more the church re-established by
himself."

De Sainte Amand says: "Much has been
said about the pride of Napoleon; on this
score we must distinguish the different per-
sons in him—the public man, and private
individual. The public man was compelled
to assume more majesty than any other sov-
ereign; the more recent the grandeur, the
more formal he was obliged to be. The
General, when he became Emperor, had to
keep at a distance those old companions in
arms who formerly were his equals and
treated him as a comrade. Familiarity
would have been an attack on his prestige,
and would have lessened his authority. In
the presence of the court he had to be a living statue, never coming down from his

pedestal. . . . . But the private individual in no way resembled the public man. When he entered his home, he laid aside his commanding gravity as a uniform, which one takes off in order to be at ease; he became affable and familiar. He joked sometimes, even somewhat noisily. He was no longer a proud potentate, a terrible conqueror; he was a good husband who rejoiced with his wife, a good father devoted to his child."

His valet, Constant, tells us: "As a father and a husband, Napoleon might have served as a model to all his subjects."

General the Count de Sagur said: "In his private relations, Napoleon was quiet and confiding, taking especial pleasure in men of honor, whose delicacy and honesty were beyond doubt, as well as irreproachable women."

Capt. F. L. Maitland, in his narration of the surrender of Bonaparte, and of his residence on board the Bellerophone, says: "It may appear surprising that a possibility

could exist of a British officer being preju-
diced in favor of one who had caused so
many calamities to his country, but to such
an extent did he possess the power of pleas-
ing, that there are few people who could
have sat at the same table with him for a
month, as did I, without feeling a sensation
of pity, allied perhaps to regret, that a man
possessed of so many fascinating qualities,
and having held so high a station in life,
should be reduced to the situation in which
I saw him." Again Captain Maitland says:
"One morning, he (Napoleon) began to
talk of his wife and child, and desired
Marchand to bring him two or three minia-
ture pictures to show me; he spoke of them
with much feeling and affection. 'I feel,'
said he, 'the conduct of the allied Sover-
eigns to be more cruel and unjustifiable towards me in that respect than in any other.
Why should they deprive me of the com-
forts of domestic society, and take from me
what must be the dearest objects of affection
to every man, my child, and the mother of

EMPEROR NAPOLEON

my child?' On his expressing himself as
above, I looked him steadily in the face to
observe whether he showed any emotion.
The tears were standing in his eyes, and the
whole of his countenance appeared evidently
under the influence of a strong feeling of
regret."

* The following are extracts from letters
written by Marie Louise to her father, the
Emperor of Austria, (1810):

"I assure you, dear papa, that the Emperor (Napoleon) has been much calumni-
ated. The more intimately one sees him,
the more one appreciates and loves him."
April 21, 1811, she wrote as follows:

" MY DEAR FATHER: You may imagine
my immense happiness. I could never believe that I could experience such joy. My
affection for my husband has increased, if
such a thing were possible, since the birth
of his son. I am still moved to tears when
I think of all the marks of tenderness he
has shown me; these marks would attach

* De Sainte Amand.

19

me to him, even if I had not already been so by reason of all of his good qualities."

In announcing the birth of his son, on returning to his room, Napoleon said: "Well, gentlemen, we have a fine vigorous boy;" and added, with profound tenderness, "My dear wife, how courageous she was, and how she suffered; I would rather have no more children, than to see her suffer so again."

Baron de Menerval in his memoirs says: "Even when most displeased, Napoleon never gave way to ridiculous passion. Great was his dignity, and greatly as he commanded respect in public audience, and under solemn circumstances, so greatly was he easy, familiar and gay in private life. An active benevolence which sprang from his heart, as much when he was vexed as when he was pleased, was felt by his own people, by his ministers, and by his officers, and his servants. In short, very often his graciousness and his favor went out to seek first some and then others, at times when they least expected it." And again, the same writer says:

" How often have I watched the Emperor keeping his son at his side, as though he were impatient to initiate him in the art of government; either seated on his favorite settee near the mantelpiece, which was decorated with two magnificent bronze busts of Scipio and Hannibal, occupied in reading some important report, or going to his writing table, which was cut out like wings, to sign a dispatch, each word of which had to be weighed; his son, seated on his knee, or pressed against his bosom, never left him. Endowed with a marvelous power of concentration, Napoleon was able at one and the same time to attend to serious matters, and to lend himself to a child's fancies. Sometimes, putting aside all his preoccupation, he would lie down on the floor at the side of his darling son, and play with him as a child himself, looking out for what would amuse him, or spare him vexation."

The Duchess d'Abrantes in her memoirs

says: "The Emperor, notwithstanding his immense genius, had a weak side, which chained him to humanity."

The following will give us an idea of Napoleon's religious views: Menerval says, " Napoleon loved his religion, and wished to honor it, and render it prosperous. This is proved by the concordat."

The Duchess d' Abrantes tells us that on Napoleon's return from Elba, while at Grenoble he was introduced to a curate. "Ah, is it you, M. le Cure," said Napoleon, "who spoke so injuriously of me every Sunday in your sermons to the cook maids?" "Ah, Mon Dieu," answered the troubled ecclesiastic, " I assure you sire——" "Oh, I know you are a good priest; go on if it amuses you. I permit liberty of worship." The poor curate remained stupefied. Napoleon seeing him so unhappy said, "Come, think no more of it, only be kind and charitable towards all. That is the true law of Jesus Christ."

Napoleon, April the 15th, 1821, in his

will declares as follows: "I die in the apostolic Roman religion, in the bosom of which I was born, more than fifty years ago."

The testimony of Napoleon to the divinity of Christ.

In a conversation with General Bertrand at St. Helena, Napoleon said as follows:

"I know men, and I tell you that Jesus Christ is not a man. Superficial minds see a resemblance between Christ and the founders of empires and the gods of other religions. That resemblance does not exist. There is between Christianity and whatever other religion the distance of infinity.

"We can say to the authors of every other religion: 'You are neither gods nor the agents of Deity. You are but missionaries of falsehood, molded from the same clay with the rest of mortals. You are made with all the passions and vices inseparable from them. Your temples and your priests proclaim your origin.' Such will be the judgment, the cry of conscience of whoever examines the gods and the temples of paganism.

" Paganism was never accepted as truth by the wise men of Greece, neither by Socrates, Pythagoras, Plato, Anaxagoras or Pericles. But on the other side, the loftiest intellects since the advent of Christianity have had faith, a living faith, a practical faith in the mysteries and the doctrines of the Gospel; not only Bossuet and Fèneleon, who were preachers, but Descartes and Newton, Leibnitz and Pascal, Corneille and Racine, Charlemagne and Louis XIV.

"Paganism is the work of man. One can here read but our imbecility. What do these gods, so boastful, know more than other mortals? These legislators, Greek or Roman? This Numa? This Lycurgus? These priests of India or of Memphis? This Confucius? This Mohammed? Absolutely nothing. There is not one among all who said anything new in reference to our future destiny, to the soul, to the essence of God, to the creation. Enter the sanctuaries of Paganism — you there find perfect chaos, a thousand contradictions, war between the gods, the immobility of sculpture, the division and rending of unity, the parceling out of the divine attributes, mutilated or denied in their essence, the sophisms of ignorance and presumption, polluted fêtes, impurity and abomination adored, all sorts of corruption festering in the thick shades, with the rotten wood, the idol and his priests. Does this honor God, or does it dishonor Him? Are these religions and these gods to be compared with Christianity?

"As for me, I say, No. I summon entire Olympus to my tribunal. I judge the gods, but am far from prostrating myself before their vain images. The gods, the legislators of India and of China, of Rome and of Athens, have nothing which can overawe me. Not that I am unjust to them; no, I appreciate them, because I know their value. Undeniably princes whose existence is fixed in the memory as an image of order and of power, as the ideal of force and beauty; such princes were no ordinary men.

" I see in Lycurgus, Numa and Mohammed only legislators, who, having the first rank in the state, have sought the best solution of the social problem; but I see nothing there which reveals divinity. They themselves have never raised their pretensions so high. As for me, I recognize the gods and these great men as beings like myself. They have performed a lofty part in their times, as I have done. Nothing announces them divine. On the contrary, there are numerous resemblances between them and myself, foibles and errors which ally them to me, and to humanity.

" It is not so with Christ. Everything in Him astonishes me. Between Him and whoever else in the world there is no possible term of comparison. He is truly a Being of Himself. His ideas and His sentiments, the truths which He announces, His manner of convincing, are not explained

either by human organization or by nature
of things.

"His birth, and the history of His life;
the profundity of His doctrines, which grap-
ple the mightiest difficulties, and which is,
of those difficulties, the most admirable solution; His gospel, His apparition, His empire, His march across the ages and the
realms, everything, is for me a prodigy, a
mystery insoluble, which plunges me into a
reverie from which I cannot escape; a mystery which is there before my eyes, a mystery which I can neither deny nor explain.
Here I see nothing human.

"The nearer I approach, the more care-
fully I examine, everything is above me,
everything remains grand — of a grandeur
which overpowers. His religion is a revela-
tion from an intelligence which certainly is
not that of man. There is there a profound
originality, which has created a series of
words and maxims before unknown. Jesus
borrowed nothing from our sciences. One
can absolutely find nowhere, but in Him

alone, the imitation or the example of His life. He is not a philosopher, since He advances by miracles, and from the commencement His disciples worshiped Him. He persuades them far more by an appeal to the heart than by any display of method and of logic. Neither did He impose upon them any preliminary studies or any knowledge of letters. All of His religion consists in *believing*.

"In fact, the sciences and philosophy avail nothing for salvation; and Jesus came into the world to reveal the mysteries of Heaven and the laws of the spirit. Also, he had nothing to do with but the soul, and to that alone He brings His Gospel. The soul is sufficient for Him, as He is sufficient for the soul. Before Him the soul was nothing. Matter and time were the masters of the world. At His voice everything returns to order. Science and philosophy become secondary. The soul has conquered its sovereignty. All the scholastic scaffolding falls, as an edifice ruined, before one single word, *faith*.

"What a master and what a word, which can effect such a revolution! With what authority does he teach men to pray? He imposes His belief, and no one, thus far, has been able to contradict Him; first, because the Gospel contains the purest morality, and also, because the doctrine which it contains of obscurity, is only the proclamation and the truth of that which exists where no eye can see, and no reason can penetrate. Who is the insensate who will say *no* to the intrepid voyager who recounts the marvels of the icy peaks which he alone has had the boldness to visit? Christ is that bold voyager. One can doubtless remain incredulous, but no one can venture to say, *It is not so.*

"Moreover consult the philosophers upon those mysterious questions, which relate to the essence of man and to the essence of religion. What is their response? Where is the man of good sense who has ever learned anything from the system of metaphysics, ancient or modern, which is not

truly a vain and pompous idealogy, without
any connection with our domestic life, with
our passions? Unquestionably, with skill
of thinking, one can seize the key of the
philosophy of Socrates and Plato; but, to
do this, it is necessary to be a metaphysician;
and moreover, with years of study, one
must possess special aptitude. But, good
sense alone, the heart, and honest spirit, are
sufficient to comprehend Christianity.

" The Christian religion is neither idealogy nor metaphysics, but a practical rule
which directs the actions of man, counsels
him, and assists him in all his conduct.
The Bible contains a complete series of
facts and of historical men, to explain time
and eternity, such as no other religion has
to offer. If this is not the true religion, one
is very excusable in being deceived, for
everything in it is grand and worthy of
God. I search in vain in history to find the
similar to Jesus Christ, or anything which
can approach the Gospel. Neither history,
nor humanity, nor the ages, nor nature, can

NAPOLEON EMPEROR AND KING

offer me anything, with which I am able to
compare it or explain it. Here everything
is extraordinary. The more I consider the
Gospel, the more I am assured there is nothing there which is not beyond the march of
events and above the human mind. Even
the impious themselves have never dared
to deny the sublimity of the Gospel, which
inspires them with a sort of compulsory
veneration. What happiness that book pro-
cures for them who believe it! What
marvels those admire there who reflect
upon it! Book unique, where the mind
finds a moral beauty before unknown, and
an idea of the Supreme superior even to
that which creation suggests. Who but
God could procure that type, that ideal of
perfection, equally exclusive and original?

"Christ, having but a few weak disciples,
was condemned to death. He dies the
object of the wrath of the Jewish priests and
the contempt of the nation, and abandoned
and denied by His own disciples.

"'They are about to take me, and to

crucify me,' said He. 'I shall be abandoned
of all the world. My chief disciple will
deny me at the commencement of my
punishment. I shall be left to the wicked.
But, then, divine justice being satisfied,
original sin being expiated by my sufferings, the bond of man and God will be
renewed, and my death will be the life of
my disciples. Then they will be more
strong without me than with me, for they
will see me rise again. I shall ascend to
the skies, and I shall send them from
heaven a spirit who will instruct them. The
spirit of the cross will enable them to under-
stand my Gospel. In fine, they will believe
it, they will preach it, and they will convert
the world.'

"And this strange promise, so aptly
called by Paul, the 'foolishness of the
Cross'; this prediction of the miserable
crucified, is literally accomplished, and the
mode of the accomplishment is, perhaps,
more prodigious than the promise.

"It is not a day nor a battle which has

32

decided it. Is it the lifetime of a man?
No, it is a war, a long combat of three
hundred years, commenced by the apostles,
and continued by their successors, and by
succeeding generations of Christians. In
this conflict all the kings and all the forces
of the earth were arrayed on one side.
Upon the other I see no army, but a mysterious energy, individuals scattered here
and there in all parts of the globe, having
no other rallying sign than a common faith
in the mysteries of the cross.

"What a mysterious symbol! The instru-
ment of the punishment of the man-God.
His disciples were armed with it. 'The
Christ,' they said, 'God has died for the
salvation of men.' What a strife, what a
tempest, these words have raised around the
humble standard of the sufferings of the
man-God! On the one side, we see rage
and all the furies of hatred and violence;
on the other, there is gentleness, moral
courage, infinite resignation. For three
hundred years spirit struggled against

brutality of sense, the conscience against despotism, the soul against the body, virtue against all the vices. The blood of Christians flowed in torrents. They died kissing the hand which slew them. The soul alone protested, while the body surrendered itself to all tortures. Everywhere Christians fell, and everywhere they triumphed.

"You speak of Cæsar, of Alexander; of their conquests, and of the enthusiasm they enkindled in the hearts of their soldiers; but can you conceive of a dead man making conquests with an army faithful and entirely devoted to his memory? My armies have forgotten me, even while living, as the Carthaginian army forgot Hannibal. Such is our power. A single battle lost crushes us, and adversity scatters our friends.

"Can you conceive of Cæsar, the eternal Emperor of the Roman senate, and from the depths of his mausoleum governing the Empire, watching over the destinies of Rome? Such is the history of the invasion and conquest of the world by Christianity.

34

Such is the power of the God of the Christians; and such is the perpetual miracle of the progress of the faith and of the government of His Church. Nations pass away, thrones crumble, but the Church remains. What is, then, the power that has protected the Church, thus assailed by the furious billows of rage, and the hostility of ages? Where is the arm which, for eighteen hundred years, has protected the Church from so many storms which have threatened to engulf it?

" In every other instance, but that of Christ, how many imperfections. Where is the character which has not yielded, vanquished by obstacles? Where is the individual who has never been governed by circumstances or places, who has never succumbed to the influence of the times, who has never computed with any customs or passions? From the first day to the last He is the same, always the same, majestic and simple, infinitely firm, and infinitely gentle.

"Truth should embrace the universe. Such is Christianity, the only religion which destroys sectional prejudice, the only one which proclaims the unity and the absolute brotherhood of the whole human family, the only one which is purely spiritual—in fine, the only one which assigns to all, without distinction, for a true country the bosom of the Creator, God. Christ proved that He was the Son of the Eternal by His disregard of Time. All His doctrines signify only one and the same thing—*Eternity*.

" It is true that Christ proposed to our faith a series of mysteries. He commands, with authority, that we should believe them, giving no other reason than those tremendous words, ' I am God.' He declares it. What an abyss He creates by that declaration between Himself and all the fabrications of religion. What audacity, what sacrilege, what blasphemy, if it were not true. I say more: The universal triumph of an affirmation of that kind, if the triumph were not really that of God Himself, would be a plausible excuse and a reason for Atheism.

"Moreover, in propounding mysteries Christ is harmonious with nature, which is profoundly mysterious. From whence do I come? Whither do I go? Who am I? Human life is a mystery in its origin, its organization, and its end. In man, and out of man, in nature, everything is mysterious. And can one wish that religion should not be mysterious? The creation and the destiny of the world are an unfathomable abyss, as also is the creation and the destiny of each individual. Christianity at least does not evade these great questions. It meets them boldly. And our doctrines are a solution of them for every one who believes.

"The Gospel possesses a secret virtue, a mysterious efficacy, a warmth which penetrates and soothes the heart. One finds in meditating upon it that which one experiences in contemplating the heavens. The Gospel is not a book; it is a living being, with an action, a power which invades everything that opposes its extension. Behold it upon this table, this Book surpassing all others. (Here the Emperor solemnly placed his hand upon it.) I never omit to read it, and every day with the same pleasure.

" Nowhere is to be found such a series of beautiful ideas, admirable moral maxims, which defile, like the battalions of a celestial army, and which produce in our soul the same emotion which one experiences in contemplating the infinite expanse of the skies, resplendent on a summer's night with all the brilliance of the stars. Not only is our mind absorbed, it is controlled, and the soul can never go astray with this Book for its guide. Once master of our spirit, the faithful Gospel loves us. God even is our friend, is our father, and truly our God. The mother has no greater care for the infant whom she nurses.

" What a proof of the divinity of Christ! With an Empire so absolute, He has but one single end, the spiritual amelioration of individuals, the purity of conscience, the union, to that which is true, the holiness of the soul.

"Christ speaks, and at once generations become His by stricter, closer ties than those of blood—by the most sacred, the most indissoluble of all unions. He lights up the flame of a love which consumes self-love, which prevails over every other love. The founders of other religions never conceived of this mystical love, which is the essence of Christianity, and is beautifully called Charity. In every attempt to effect this thing, namely, to make Himself beloved, man deeply feels his own impotence. So that Christ's greatest miracle undoubtedly is the reign of *Charity*.

" I have so inspired multitudes that they would die for me. God forbid that I should form any comparison between the enthusiasm of the soldier and the Christian Charity, which are as unlike as their cause. But, after all, my presence was necessary; the lightning of my eye, my voice, a word from me—then the sacred fire was kindled in their hearts. I do, indeed, possess the secret of this magical power which lifts the soul, but I could never impart it to any one. None of my generals ever learned it from me; nor have I the means of perpetuating my name and love for me in the hearts of men, and to effect these things without physical means.

" Now that I am at St. Helena, now that I am alone, chained upon this rock, who fights and wins empires for me? Who are the courtiers of my misfortune? Who thinks of me? Who makes efforts for me in Europe? Where are my friends? Yes, two or three, whom your fidelity immortalizes, you share, you console my exile."

(Here the voice of the Emperor trembled with emotion, and for a moment he was silent; he then continued.)

" Yes, our life once shone with all the brilliance of the diadem and the throne; and yours, Bertrand, reflected that splendor, as the dome of the Invalides, gilt by us, reflects the rays of the sun. But disasters

40

came; the gold gradually became dim. The ruin of misfortune and outrage with which I am daily deluged has effaced all the brightness. We are mere lead now, General Bertrand, and soon I shall be in my grave.

"Such is the fate of great men. So it was with Cæsar, and Alexander; and I, too, am forgotten. And the name of a conqueror and an Emperor is a college theme. Our exploits are tasks given to pupils by their tutors, who sit in judgment upon us, awarding censure or praise. And mark what is soon to become of me. Assassinated by the English oligarchy, I die before my time; and my dead body, too, must return to the earth, to become food for worms. Behold the destiny near at hand of him who has been called the Great Napoleon. What an abyss between my deep misery and the eternal reign of Christ, which is proclaimed, loved, adored, and which is extending all over the earth. Is this to die? Is it not rather to live? The death of Christ. It is the death of God.

41

" General Bertrand, if you do not perceive that Jesus Christ is God, very well; then I did wrong to make you a General."

NAPOLEON AT ST. HELENA

THE GRAVE OF BONAPARTE

On a lone barren isle where the wild roaring billows
  Assail the stern rock and the loud tempests rave,
The hero lies still, while the dew-drooping willows,
  Like fond weeping mourners, leaned over the grave.
The lightnings may flash, and the loud thunder rattle,
  He heeds not, he hears not, he's free from all pain;
He sleeps his last sleep, he has fought his last battle,
  No sound can awake him to glory again.

Oh, shade of the Mighty, where now are the legions
  That rushed but to conquer when thou led'st them
     on?
Alas, they have perished in far hilly regions,
  And all save the fame of their triumph is gone.
The tempest may sound, and the loud cannon rattle,
  They heed not, they hear not, they're free from all
    pain;
They sleep their last sleep, they have fought their last
  battle,
  No sound can awake them to glory again.

Yet, spirit immortal, the tomb cannot bind thee,
  For like thine own eagle that soared to the sun,
Thou springest from bondage, and leavest behind thee
  A name, which before thee no mortal had won.
Though nations may combat and war's thunders
  rattle,
  No more on thy steed wilt thou sweep o'er the
    plain;
Thou sleep'st thy last sleep, thou hast fought thy last
  battle,
  No sound can awake thee to glory again.

www.ingramcontent.com/pod-product-compliance
Lightning Source LLC
Chambersburg PA
CBHW021433090426
42739CB00009B/1465